Traverse Theatre Company

This is Paradise

by Michael John O'Neill

First performed at the Traverse Theatre, Edinburgh,
on 5th August 2022

A Traverse Theatre Company Commission

Company

KATE   Amy Molloy

Director   Katherine Nesbitt
Set and Costume Designer   Lulu Tam
Lighting Designer   Colin Grenfell
Sound Designer   Danny Krass
Dramaturg   Eleanor White
Associate Lighting Designer   Jason Addison
Associate Sound Designer   Richard Bell

Production Manager   Kevin McCallum
Chief Electrician   Renny Robertson
Head of Stage   Jamie Hayes
Stage Technician   Dave Bailey
Stage Technician   Fi Elliott
Stage Manager   Hannah Gallardo-Parsons

Biographies

Amy Molloy (KATE)

Amy's work at the Edinburgh Fringe includes solo show *Cotton Fingers* at Summerhall (2019), for which she won a Lustrum Award. The play was listed as one of the best shows of the Fringe by *The Stage* that year.

She also performed and produced solo show *Tea Set* by Gina Moxley, at the Pleasance Courtyard (2015), making Lyn Gardner's 'Top Tickets of the Fringe'.

After helping develop and perform the play last year, this year sees Amy return to the Traverse as Kate in *This is Paradise* after its first successful outing in 2021 in Traverse 1.

Other theatre work includes the award-winning *Cyprus Avenue* (Royal Court/Abbey Theatre/Public Theater NYC and Mac Belfast runs 2016–2019) in which Amy originated the role of Julie, playing opposite Stephen Rea. The play was listed in the top fifty plays of the twenty-first century by *The Guardian*, and the film of the play aired on BBC Four and iPlayer in 2020.

She has performed at the National Theatre (London) in *Translations*, at the Abbey Theatre and BAM Harvey NYC in *John Gabriel Borkman*, and performed for renowned Irish production companies such as Druid, Pan Pan, Prime Cut and Bruiser.

Film and TV includes *Animals* by Emma Jane Unsworth, *Love Without Walls*, *71*, short film *Bound* (Best Female Actor nomination, RHIFF), *Call the Midwife*, *Bloodlands*, *The Fall* and *Cyprus Avenue*.

Michael John O'Neill (Writer)

Michael John O'Neill is a Northern Irish playwright, dramaturg and theatre producer based in Scotland. In 2019 Michael became the inaugural recipient of the Bruntwood Prize's Original New Voice Award for his play *Akedah*. In 2020 his digital short *Sore Afraid* was produced by National Theatre of Scotland, Citizens Theatre, and BBC Scotland, and his audio short *Part of that World* was produced by Pitlochry Festival Theatre. In 2021 his play *This is Paradise* was commissioned by the Traverse Theatre and won the Popcorn Writing Award. He is developing new plays with the Almeida Theatre (as part of the Genesis New Writers' Programme), Lyric Theatre Belfast and Rage Productions Mumbai, Hampstead Theatre (as Writer on Attachment), National Theatre of Scotland (as Writer on Attachment), and Playwrights' Studio, Scotland (as a New Playwrights' Award Winner). His work as a theatre producer includes as Artistic Producer of the Tron Theatre (2014-2020), where he founded the Tron's new work department, and commissioned and produced Isobel McArthur's *Pride and Prejudice* (*Sort Of)*.

Katherine Nesbitt (Director)

Katherine Nesbitt is a director and dramaturg from Belfast, and is an Associate Artist of the Traverse Theatre and an Associate Director of the National Theatre Connections Festival 2022. Work for the Traverse includes as Associate Director on *Mouthpiece* by Kieran Hurley, directed by Orla O'Loughlin (2019, 2020) and JMK Regional Assistant Director bursary recipient on *Swallow* by Stef Smith, directed by Orla O'Loughlin (2015). Other work includes as a director on *Class Act* (2019), as a script reader for the Traverse since 2016, and on a number of works-in-progress and script development days.

Other recent directing work includes *Parts Per Million* by Gary McNair (Guildhall School of Music and Drama), *Telegraph Hill* by Alice Malseed (View From Here), *Wee Buns* by Caitlin Magnall-Kearns (Lyric Theatre Belfast), *The Present* by Stef Smith (National Theatre of Scotland/BBC Scotland Scenes for Survival, Traverse in association), *Jade City* (Bunker

Theatre). Other Associate Director credits include *The Open House* by Will Eno (Michael Boyd, Bath Theatre Royal Ustinov Studio). Assistant Director credits include *Holy Sh!t* by Alexis Zegerman (Indhu Rubasingham, Kiln Theatre) and *iHo* by Tony Kushner (Michael Boyd, Hampstead Theatre).

Katherine is a member of the Lincoln Center Theater Directors' Lab. She was a Finalist for the JMK Award 2021 and the Sir Peter Hall Director Award 2021. She has worked as a script reader for National Theatre of Scotland, Lyric Theatre Belfast, Theatre Uncut Award, Tron Theatre and the Papatango Prize.

Lulu Tam (Set and Costume Designer)

Lulu Tam is a scenographer who likes to explore materials, body, and space in performance. She works nationally and internationally and has been actively engaged in renowned festivals; Prague Quadrennial of Performance Design and Space 2011 and 2019, London Art Biennale 2015. She was a finalist of the Linbury Prize and the winner of Taking the Stage supported by British Council Ukraine in 2015, and was a selected designer at World Stage Design 2017, Taipei. She is now a lecturer at Central School of Speech and Drama.

Colin Grenfell (Lighting Designer)

Work for the Traverse includes *Still*, *The Devil Masters*, *Pandas*, *On the Exhale*.

Other work includes *Pride and Prejudice* * (*Sort Of)* (Criterion Theatre), *Oh When the Saints* (Perth Theatre), *Leopards* (Rose Theatre), *Christmas Dinner* (Royal Lyceum Theatre, Edinburgh), *The King of Hell's Palace* (Hampstead Theatre), *Gypsy*, *Macbeth*, *The Cherry Orchard*, *Kes* (Royal Exchange Theatre, Manchester), *Black Watch*, *365*, *Men Should Weep*, *The Bacchae*, *Granite* (National Theatre of Scotland), *Tao of Glass* (Manchester International Festival), *An Improbable Musical*, *Still No Idea*, *70 Hill Lane*, *Coma*, *The Paper Man*, *Spirit* (Improbable), *A Christmas Carol* (Liverpool Everyman, Spymonkey) *Tamburlaine* (RSC), *The Mentor* (Theatre Royal Bath and Vaudeville Theatre), *Lost Without Words*, *Lifegame*, *Theatre of Blood* (Improbable/Royal National Theatre), *The Village Social* (National Theatre of Wales), *Beauty and the Beast* (MCA, Chicago, Abrons New York, Adelaide Festival), *The Caretaker* (Liverpool Everyman, Trafalgar Studios, BAM), *A Midsummer Night's Dream*, *Half Life*, *The Mother*, *Forever Yours*, *Marie-Lou*, *Wild Goose Dreams*, *Xmas Eve* (Theatre Royal Bath), *Cat on a Hot Tin Roof* (Theatr Clwyd, Best Lighting Award at the 2017 Wales Theatre Awards), *The Elephant Man* (Best Design CATS Award), *The Hanging Man* (Best Design TMA Awards).

Danny Krass (Sound Designer)

Danny Krass is a sound designer and composer for theatre, radio and podcasts. Work for the Traverse includes *The Artist Man and the Mother Woman* by Morna Pearson, *Swallow* by Stef Smith, *Quiz Show* by Rob Drummond, *Meet Me at Dawn* by Zinnie Harris, and *Letters to Morrisey* by Gary McNair.

Other recent productions include *Christmas Dinner* by Rob Evans (Royal Lyceum Theatre), *I Am Tiger* by Oliver Emanuel (Perth Theatre/Imaginate), *Don Juan* by Grant O'Rourke after Molière (Perth Theatre), *The Secret Garden* by Ros Sydney (Redbridge Arts).

Danny was the Composer and Sound Designer for *The System* by Ben Lewis for BBC Radio 4, which received a Prix Europa award in 2021 for Best Radio Fiction Series. He is the lead artist for *Earwig: Sonic Theatre Podcasts* in association with the Tron Theatre. Both series are going into their second seasons in 2022 and can be found wherever you get your podcasts.

Traverse Theatre Company

The Traverse is a champion of performance, experience and discovery. Enabling people to access and engage with theatre is our fundamental mission, and we want our work to represent, speak to and be seen by the broadest cross section of society. We are specialists in revealing untold perspectives in innovative ways. This is our role as Scotland's new writing theatre and a commitment that drives each strand of our work.

Our year-round programme bursts with new stories, live and digital performances that challenge, inform and entertain our audiences. We empower artists and audiences to make sense of the world today, providing a safe space to question, learn, empathise and – crucially – encounter different people and experiences. Conversation and the coming together of groups are central to a democratic society, and we champion equal expression and understanding for the future of a healthy national and international community.

The Traverse would not exist without our overarching passion for developing new stories and embracing the unexplored. We work with bold voices and raw talent – with an emphasis on the Scottish-based – to create the art, artists, and performances that can be seen on our platforms year-round. We invest in ideas and support individuals to push boundaries by placing them at the centre of their own practice, and through projects like Class Act, Traverse Young Writers, and First Stages the continual relationship between artist development and performance can be seen in powerful action.

We aim for the timely stories and creative programmes that start life with us to have a global impact, through tours, co-productions, digital life, and translations. We are critically acclaimed and recognised the world over for our originality and artistic risk, which we hope will create some of the most talked-about plays, productions, directors, writers, and actors for years to come.

The Traverse's commitment to bringing new and bold storytelling to global audiences is amplified in Edinburgh each August, when international audiences make the Traverse programme – often referred to as the 'beating heart of the Fringe' – their first port of call in a city overflowing with entertainment offerings.

Our past successes drive our present and future direction, in the knowledge that our unique ability to nurture new talent and engage audiences through ambitious storytelling has never been more crucial in creating and sustaining a vibrant theatre landscape that reflects and challenges the world today.

Find out more about our work: traverse.co.uk

With thanks

The Traverse extends grateful thanks to all those who collaborate with us and support our work, including those who prefer to remain anonymous.

Traverse Theatre Supporters:

DIAMOND
Alan & Penny Barr
Katie Bradford
Kirsten Lamb
David Rodgers

PLATINUM
Judy & Steve
Angus McLeod
Iain Millar
Mike & Carol Ramsay

GOLD
Roger & Angela Allen
Carola Bronte-Stewart
Iona Hamilton

SILVER
Bridget M Stevens
Allan Wilson
Gaby Thomson
Chris & Susan Gifford
Lesley Preston

BRONZE
Barbara Cartwright
Alex Oliver & Duncan Stephen
Patricia Pugh
Beth Thomson
Julia & David Wilson
Stephanie & Neil
Drs Urzula & Michael Glienecke
Viv Phillips
Jon Best

TRAVERSE THEATRE PRODUCTION SUPPORTERS

Cotterell & Co
Paterson SA Hairdressing

TRUSTS, FOUNDATIONS AND GRANTS

Anderson Anderson & Brown Charitable Initiative
Arnold Clark Community Fund
Backstage Trust
British Council Scotland and Creative Scotland: UK in Japan 2019–20
Bruce Wake Charitable Trust
Cruden Foundation
D'Oyly Carte Charitable Trust
Dr David Summers Charitable Trust
Garrick Charitable Trust
Harold Hyam Wingate Foundation
Heritage Fund
Idlewild Trust
John Thaw Foundation
Murdoch Forrest Charitable Trust
Museum Galleries Scotland
RKT Harris Charitable Trust
The David and June Gordon Memorial Trust
The Foyle Foundation
The Great Britain Sasakawa Foundation
The JMK Trust
The JTH Charitable Trust
The Leche Trust
The Mackintosh Foundation
The McGlashan Charitable Trust
The Nancie Massey Charitable Trust
The Nimar Charitable Trust
The Noël Coward Foundation
The Paul Hamlyn Foundation
The Robert Haldane Smith Charitable Foundation
The Robertson Trust
The Royal Edinburgh Military Tattoo
The Russell Trust
The Teale Charitable Trust
The Turtleton Charitable Trust
The William Syson Foundation
The W M Mann Foundation
Theatres Trust
Unity Theatre Trust
Visit Scotland

GRANT FUNDERS

The Traverse Theatre is funded by Creative Scotland and The City of Edinburgh Council. We have received additional support from the Scottish Government's Performing Arts Venue Relief Fund and Adapt and Thrive, part of the Scottish Government's Community and Third Sector Recovery Programme and delivered in partnership by Firstport, Corra Foundation, SCVO, Just Enterprise, Community Enterprise and Social Investment Scotland.

ALBA | CHRUTHACHAIL

Traverse Theatre (Scotland) is a Limited Company (SC076037) and a Scottish Charity (SC002368) with its Registered Office at 10 Cambridge Street, Edinburgh, Scotland, EH1 2ED.

Traverse Theatre

The Company

This is Paradise

Michael John O'Neill is a playwright, dramaturg and theatre producer from the north coast of Ireland. In 2019 Michael became the inaugural recipient of the Bruntwood Prize's Original New Voice Award for his play *Akedah*. In 2020 his digital short *Sore Afraid* was produced by National Theatre of Scotland, Citizens Theatre and BBC Scotland, and his audio short *Part of that World* was produced by Pitlochry Festival Theatre. In 2021 his play *This is Paradise* was commissioned by the Traverse Theatre and won the Popcorn Writing Award. He is developing new plays with the Almeida Theatre (as part of the Genesis New Writers' Programme), Lyric Theatre Belfast and Rage Productions Mumbai, Hampstead Theatre (as Writer on Attachment), National Theatre of Scotland (as Writer on Attachment), and Playwrights' Studio, Scotland (as a New Playwrights' Award Winner). His work as a theatre producer includes as Artistic Producer of the Tron Theatre (2014–2020), where he founded the Tron's new work department, and commissioned and produced Isobel McArthur's *Pride and Prejudice** (**Sort Of*).

MICHAEL JOHN O'NEILL

This is Paradise

faber

First published in 2022
by Faber and Faber Limited
The Bindery, 51 Hatton Garden
London EC1N 8HN

Typeset by Brighton Gray
Printed and bound in the UK by CPI Group (Ltd), Croydon CR0 4YY

A CIP record for this book
is available from the British Library

978–0–571–37604–9

2 4 6 8 10 9 7 5 3

Acknowledgements

This play would not be as it is now were it not for George Aza-Selinger, Marina Carr, Lily Levinson, Isobel McArthur, Christina McClements, Lucianne McEvoy, Kei Miller, Amy Molloy, Katherine Nesbitt, Gareth Nicholls, Iris O'Neill, Jan O'Neill, John O'Neill, Linden O'Neill, Rosa O'Neill, Imogen Sarre, Eleanor White, Rob Willoughby, Dinah Wood, Anatomy at Summerhall, Creative Scotland, Faber, National Theatre of Scotland, Only Skin at SWG3, Popcorn Group, SCRATCH at The Arches, Student Housing Association Co-op (SHAC), Traverse Theatre, and anonymous readers at Playwrights' Studio Scotland and the Royal Court.

This is Paradise was first performed at the Traverse Theatre, Edinburgh, on 5 August 2022, with the following cast:

Kate Amy Molloy

Director Katherine Nesbitt
Set and Costume Designer Lulu Tam
Lighting Designer Colin Grenfell
Sound Designer Danny Krass
Dramaturg Eleanor White

for Linden and for Rosa

Character

Kate
thirty-four

Setting

Ireland
1998 and before 1998

THIS IS PARADISE

Act One

Here we are, having a sit.
  And then she goes:

To think

so many years later

some wee girl I don't even know

would be calling me about you

calling me

on Good Friday

on this Good Friday

with everything

with my body and my Brendy

both sat here

watching the news saying peace has arrived

with my body waiting to be seen and poked and pried apart
at Belfast City Hospital

and some wee girl

your latest child bride

she's calling me

she's not even introducing herself

is going to me

saying

'Diver isn't answering my calls'

crying

crying 'please

I don't know what to do'

and I'm hearing her in my own voice

but from before

from that day we ate peaches on the train.

Do you remember that, Diver?

I have it

somehow clearer now

that picture

the wet yellow

your fingers sticking to mine

the heat in the carriage

even with every window cracked

and the heat

fuck me the heat that summer

going from town to town along the coast of Liguria

the water on one side of me

and you always on the other

either direction, a clear expanse.

Remembering that

so early in our time together

must have been 1980

just a week

just a few days

no doubt running from some bad fellas after you back home

sure there was always bad fellas after you

was always someone you were letting down.

And then our last night in that twin room in Pisa

twin room

booking error

but the manager's look

these two travelling together?

These two?

You barely clinging on to your thirties

and me

fuck

ing

hell

sure me.

His eyes on me.

Thinking Jesus what age is that wee girl?

Not that he's saying anything

not with your charm.

I'm stood back

a bystander for once

but still feeling it

the force of you

pushing through that solid heat

the poor guy

that feeling

desperate to yield

to appease you

sure he is

to give you everything

but the twin room is all they have

so you relent

take the key

and scrawl your name

Diver

you scrawl it in his book

Diver

like you scrawled it in mine

across the margins

in those big cartoon loops and tails

Diver

and then after dinner

alone with the two single beds and the floor-fan whirring

suddenly you're gone from me

so sullen

forcing me to take you in my fists and wring it out of you

that you've met someone

ahhh fuck

again

ahhh fuck, Katey

just before we left Belfast

so this would be the last time

fucking stay where you are

the last time

we'd be doing whatever it was we've been doing

and I says is this the last last time?

Or is it the last time like last time was the last time?

Then a laugh

was that you, or me, I can't

I can't separate us out

and then silence

which was most definitely both of us

and then me

breaking it

me saying

   Beat.

'I think I'm pregnant, Diver'

but saying it flat

(*Quick, quiet.*) 'I think I'm pregnant'

like I was asking you to hold my purse

so I wasn't sure if you even heard me

because you looked through me

and said maybe it being separate beds was a blessing

and looking anywhere but my awful body

saying and saying you love me

don't

that you

don't touch me

that

don't

and we fought until we didn't

laid down

shaking with anger

each in our own bed

the river rising between us

and in the night I know I've bled.

    Beat.

And in the morning

before we handed back the key

your skin still tasted of peach.

*

'Katey, he kept saying if I left him

sure I don't like to say it

    Beat.

(*Whispered.*) saying he would end it

you know, like end himself.

I thought maybe he was joking.

And then I did leave him

because I had to

   Beat.

And now he hasn't answered the phone in two weeks.

I don't know what to do.

He told me what would happen if I left.'

   Beat.

When me and husband Brendy were not yet even me and
husband Brendy

but instead just me and the fella

when we were in that kind of mood

raking over the names of those we shifted before we took to
shifting each other to a permanent end

I would talk to Brendy about my years with Diver

first in Belfast

always moving

always hustling

and then when it got too hot for him in the city

that year together seeing no one

holed up in that ridiculous caravan on the north coast.

Portbenoney.

We went there

1986

I was

twenty-two

and Diver was

I think we did his forty-fifth in that caravan

a scone with a tea light sliding off it.

Me anchoring a party hat around his chin

him too gone to notice.

He was gone from himself a lot by that point

made it easier for me to finally slip away I think.

Brendy

he was always grinning and saying he wanted to go up
there some day

to that nowhere town by the sea

saying Diver was probably still in that caravan

saying he was probably a proper crusty now

covered in barnacles and harvesting seaweed

(because he's whimsical, is Brendy)

saying he wanted to thank this madman from my before

this shady grifter who talked about the carnage of our city
like it was a thing of beauty

this man who called himself Diver

and thank him

sincerely

for taking a machete to my expectations.

Which suited Brendy just fine.

I never told him about the worst stuff.

That shape Diver's face would take

when I stole a glance back at him in the station toilets

me standing guard while he was sat on the piss-wet floor
putting that stuff in between his toes.

I want Brendy

I want for him not to have to hold any of that in his head.

Brendy is not breaking.

Not like I am.

Brendy comes from a big family of Brendy admirers.

Only boy, youngest, four sisters.

Sturdy, dependable women. At least two of them pregnant
at any given moment.

And Brendy

that fella

fuck me

he prides himself on having washed the pots and pans
before we even sit down to eat.

He votes Alliance.

When he's going about the house

doing his little tasks

It is killing Kate to admit this.

he whistles

even when he knows I can hear him

I mean

Jesus wept.

Beat.

Even now

I'm not sure I love him.

At least, not the way I tell him I love him

so he won't worry himself.

But I love how he fears me.

I love how he thinks that being good to me is why I stay.

And I love how he does not know

that to have what we have

to have made it this far

every part of me is breaking.

   Beat.

When I'm good and ready

I says to Brendy about Diver being missing

I says

'I'm afraid for him, Brendy'

and then we talk half the night about it

and I can tell when we're done

and Brendy is off whistling at the laundry

that he has happily tuned out the part where I said I was
going back to Portbenoney the next morning

to find Diver

or whatever is left of him.

   Beat.

I don't sleep

I've not been sleeping for weeks

not since I first started feeling this pain.

Kate touches her abdomen.

And then the next day, finally, thank God

and sure enough

here's Brendy

here's him seeing my bag in the hall

here's him on at me

immediately

'You can't go anywhere

not now

not like this.'

Kate nearly touches her abdomen again, then moves on.

Here's him banging his fist on the dresser

like he's got any violence in him

oh ho, bangs his fist again so he does

big fearsome Brendy

bangs it and then knocks that nice picture of Mummy and Daddy off the wall.

And I look down at it

see them

in the garden

not long before Daddy went last year

went so slowly and then so fast

and in the background, City Hospital looking close

like it's waiting for him

'I'm saying you can't go.'

'Why not? I'm signed off.'

'The twelve-week scan.'

Kate looks away.

'What if you miss it? What about the pains?'

'Brendy, that's not till Tuesday.'

'You're not doing this.'

'Oh am I not?

Thank fuck you were here to tell me

sure there was me half out the door.'

I see now this red mark down the side of his face

he does this thing I hate

he does this thing where he scratches himself

when he's stressed

or upset

goes off in private to do it

off by himself like some bad dog.

'Let her, let the girlfriend'

'She's not his girlfriend

they broke up

she left him'

'Aye, just like you did.'

'So?'

'So . . . so . . . you've been shot of him ten years

he is no longer your responsibility

she's more recent, let her deal with it.'

'She's just a child, Brendy.'

'Isn't that what he prefers?

  Beat. Brendy knows he has overstepped.

'Brendy.

All I am doing is I'm getting on a train

getting off again

enjoying the stroll and the sea air

and then I'm stopping by Diver's, knocking on the door

just see if he answers.

If he's there, grand.

If there's no answer

  Beat.

either way it's straight back to sea air and strolling

and then the next morning the train and home to you.

Brendy, I am saying I will be back through that door
tomorrow

early

so we can get to your parents for Easter lunch

see the whole crowd, your sisters, the kids'

'Right, I'll come'

'No'

  Beat.

I say that too quickly.

We both notice.

  Beat.

27

And then he says

'What am I supposed to do?'

just whining he is now

'Fucking

I don't know, Brendy

throw a party

it's peace in our time.'

I look at the TV

outside Stormont

some big round boys from the order are doing an angry
march up the hill and down again

but it's perestroika, lads

we'll neither be up nor down ever again

didn't anyone tell you?

'What if'

Brendy catches himself.

Go on

you coward

go on and say it

'What if'

He looks to me as breathless as them sweating protestants
on the telly

thin lips grasping for a word that does not exist

and so finally he says

'What if while you're gone

it happens.'

    Pause.

(*Quiet.*) 'And you lose it.'

It.

No name to it.

Just it.

'I thought "it" wasn't a word we said in this house? I thought you had a better word. Your gift to me.'

'That's not fair, Kate'

'Fair.'

I pluck this

this absurd

I pluck this

that sound

that

'Fair'

I pluck it from the air between us

right as it's wisping into nothing

I take it back and I wrestle it until it's loud again

and then I push it into the middle of Brendy's chest

and he doesn't cry out

even as the shriek of it cuts his jumper to ribbons

and cuts the flesh

and cuts the sinew

and the hard bone

29

and I wait for him to meet my eyes again

I wait for him to see the river behind them

see it rising to take me to Diver

all the way out there in the crush of the river's mouth

where I belong

because before

   A feeling builds in Kate.

before

before Diver

before

before

   That feeling is pressed back down.

'I tell you what'

I say

'if *it* happens

then it's happened.

And you can just be thankful, can't you, Brendy?

That *it* happened in a nothing town by the sea

miles from everything "fair" you're looking after up here in the new world

and then you won't even need to worry about it

not at all.

And that's my gift to you. Husband.'

   Pause.

And then I go and call a taxi to the train station

and I wait in the hall for a full hour until it comes.
'Sorry, my love
It's bumper to bumper out there
half the roads closed
for these politicals
to go and come back
and be safe from us savages
I don't know
I don't know
where are we off to?'

Act Two

I'd forgotten how to do this.

Diver.

How to think about you.

That tear above your lip

the slow way you close your eyes

the fucking length of you, boy

Christ you went a country mile heel to pate.

I remember the weeks you didn't come home

I remember how alive you were in the right company

a visit from a foreign dignitary

playing host as if you were part of something

chatting up some German girl and her German girlfriend

Red Army Faction types

heavy boots and khaki coats

or stroking beards with a fella claiming to be a second
cousin to Malcom X

or sometimes only with me

when an idea got loose in about you

and fuck there was no stopping you then

you beast you.

One night

one of them nights we were hiding in your nana's place in the Holylands

you were after disappointing some of them bad fellas again

and sure there's the woman herself now

Nana

in that green kimono you'd bought her at St George's market

half-cut as usual she is

laughing and telling me stories

saying to me

'a wee hallion

only ever good for breaking things'

telling me when you were growing

you'd found out how to make nitroglycerine

you'd make it in her kitchen

and sleep with it under your bed

telling me you were stretching out so quickly them days

you'd just keel over from time to time

if you got up too fast.

Your nana.

God love her.

She'd be in the other room

smoking out the window

that window with the bottom corner smashed out

and she'd hear this almighty clatter

and she'd come through and find you on the floor

all her good china broken about you

find you there in the middle of it, weeping

but with your eyes closed

like you weren't awake

and she'd kneel and just watch

astounded

these tears

sure they were pelting out of you

and your nana sat there like she was after lifting her head
from prayer

only to discover the mother woman herself

the best of us

like they found her down in Knock

weeping blood and oil and commodified debt.

*

(*Confused, loud.*) 'Where'd you say you are going?'

This fella in the ticket office scratches his chin.

'Portbenoney' I says.

He pulls out a sheet of paper and peers down a list.

    Beat. Kate grows impatient.

'Portbenoney.'

'Aye, I know where you're on about now.'

'When's the next train?'

'Never.'

'Excuse me?'

'Decommissioned. The station

aye

years ago.

Closest I can get you is Coleraine

and then you'll need to be getting a bus

but you'll want to check if they're running over the Easter weekend.'

'Can you not tell me?'

The ticket office fella chuckles.

'Oh no, sure that's a whole other subsidiary does the buses.'

I take my seat on board the train.

I should sleep

but I can't

these last few weeks

I'd not been sleeping, I'd not

so I'd been out walking

trying to get somewhere

I don't know

somewhere I went once in a dream

back when all of this was a dream.

Every night

slipping away

as soon as I'm hearing Brendy's breath turn soft beside me

out I am

walking

miles and miles

to the city

to the river

going

not sleeping

I can't sleep

the racket of them lorries

rattling by

loaded up with our new peace

the racket of my body

the noise of it

breaking

always

and the waiting

the waiting they're making me do

when there's not an inch of waiting left in me

in any of us

all the letters

all the calls

all the delays

'I'm sorry, Mrs Regan, if there's no blood we can't get you an emergency appointment'

all this waiting

all to be seen and scanned and pried apart

to be told what I already know

that I am breaking

I have always been breaking

it is as simple as that.

And we are such simple things.

   Beat.

Before all this

me and Brendy

we got to trying a bit later than would have been ideal.

He was the one who wanted it

and I

I knew this world around us

like he couldn't

I knew it was breaking just as much as me.

Bringing a wee one into that

sure I was in no rush.

But seeing Brendy

seeing all them nieces and nephews

seeing his want for it

the pressure of that

I stumbled

I forgot myself

I started thinking in the wrong direction is what I did

and the feeling takes hold

and then them on the news

they started on about peace

and how we're in a 'peace process' now

and I thought

I feel so fucking silly

but I thought they meant real peace

fucking hell, Katey

I thought they meant that even my body

it might stop

breaking

for one second even

and in that thought

suddenly

I was like

   A rush hits Kate.

fuck me I'm getting into my thirties and

fuck me my mum had me when she was eighteen

and then here's me

not even sure I could get that way

because I thought I was

that night in the twin room

when I said I was

and Diver

he

but it didn't matter

because in the morning his skin still tasted of peach

even if mine tasted of ash

I was so late

and then I wasn't

his skin

his heat

and then the amount of near-misses over the years

the way I behaved

so when the second stick was in my hand saying exactly
what the first stick had said

and Brendy is on to me like

'Fucking yes. Fucking put a notice in the paper'

and I'm back to him saying

'take it easy

aren't you supposed to wait a bit?'

the peach

his skin

and Brendy, he's saying

'Wait?

Wait?'

and looking at me with wild eyes

eyes that scared even me

and he's not wrong

I'm saying

about the waiting

you look

you see

there's not an inch of waiting left in anyone round here.

*

Before you, Diver

I'm saying

before

before you there was nothing.

I tell a lie.

Before you there had only been Joseph.

Big Joe!

Told me I was better looking than all the girls in Year
Eleven, even Lizzie McClune who danced with tap shoes
and played piano to grade six.

Big Joe the goalie, stopped still on the field while the ball
sails past his head cos there's wee Kate Regan walking on
by.

Went to the movies, a gang of us

spat a Malteser on Big Joe's lap

just because.

And Big Joe

he let it melt into his jeans.

Afterwards says, could he see me again tomorrow?

Big Joe scoring his name on to wee Kate's diary with a
compass then a biro.

From Paris

a school trip

sends me a letter then another letter

says I was better looking than all the French girls he was
getting off with. What was the weather like back home?
Would I promise not to go with anyone else until he got back?

And then Big Joe

lying there

sure get up now, Joe

big lump just lying down where they dragged him up from
the water

after acting the maggot on some ould bridge and taking a
header into the Seine

Big Joe lying there

lazy get

with his neck bent wrong

bent full sideways

his body broken on the river.

'The Pont Neuf bridge' says the article in the *Belfast
Telegraph*

third paragraph down

beloved son, promising student.

And then comes one last letter

after

I'm saying it didn't arrive till weeks later

I'm saying the funeral had happened

(or at least that's what they told me

sure, I didn't go)

I'm saying he was in the ground

and then I'm sat there on the stairs and it's this letter

must have sent it the day it happened, or the day before

and it took this long to arrive

and there's Big Joe asking me,

saying to me

saying 'Kate, why haven't you written me back?

Have you gone off me, Kate?'

(*Angry.*) Daring to ask that

to say that to me

when he wasn't even alive anymore.

   Beat.

I stuffed that letter in my bag and I carried it with me everywhere.

   Beat.

Daddy was pure raging I didn't go to the funeral.

'What are Big Joe's big mummy and big daddy going to think?

Love of their big boyo's short life and she can't even be bothered to come say her goodbyes.

She hasn't cried once, not once.

And already going out she is

every night of the week

out there with the scum of the earth.

Christ, wee girl

I don't even know who you are anymore.'

And I felt the breath rush out of me

and when it came back in

you came with it, Diver.

Not a heartbeat between Joe and you

but there was more than twenty years between the two of us.

I was sixteen that first time

even younger than your latest child bride

did you know that?

I think you did

sick fuck you boy you so you were

but sure, that's why I liked you.

After Joe

someone who wanted me breaking.

Met you at a party I shouldn't have been at.

Fully pixelated I was.

You marched right up

you says to me

you says you'd seen me

seen me quite a bit

cutting about with some pal with long legs

paused thinking on her name

'Shonagh?'

Kate and Shonagh, the Gilnahirk Girls.

Kate and Shonagh who sliced each other's hair in Shonagh's
mummy's kitchen when they were six and seven.

Kate and Shonagh who between them knew all the bad words.

Kate and Shonagh that were just the worst the Girl Guides had ever seen

smoking over by the fence with the lads who still lived at home but wore their hair long and wrassled with each other just as Jacob wrassled with the big man and lost and always lost and still is losing

you said to me 'hold my hand now, Katey.

I know you.

I know exactly who you are.

I have always known you.

You and me

we are such simple things.'

And we took me from the party

left Big Joe bent backwards on the floor

and we brought me to the bar across the road

where you sat there staring at me for the longest time

waiting for me to bolt

but I didn't

I wouldn't

and eventually I says

'Here, fella'

and you says something about having just been at Seamus Costello's funeral

and I says I have no idea who that is

and you said

'imagine if this place blew up right now

right on top of us'

and I looked bored

and you said 'no really

here

let me show you'

getting me just where you wanted me

guiding me with a light hand on the lower back.

The bodyguard's touch.

'Move a little to your left.

A little more

That's it. Stay right there. Take a seat.

Now don't move an inch.

It's

say it's under this table here. When it goes

   Diver makes the sound of an explosion.

You sit right there and you'll be fine.

Remember when you came in with mud on your shoes and
your mummy clipped your ear too hard?

Remember the way the hallway stretched out and your
blood felt hot? The hair on your skin all damp.

That's the worst you'll feel when it goes off.

You sit there and you'll be fine.'

And I took a sip of something shocking

I was always for drinking something shocking back then

and I did you a sideways look and says to you

'What about all them?'

'What about them, Katey?'

'Will they'

'You see that fella there?'

   Kate turns to look.

'Now don't look.

You'll make him shy.

You saw him on your way in

He eyed you. Up and down. Smiled half a hungry lip at you.
He's gone. You understand? The roof is coming down and
he's gone.'

'What's his name?'

'Come on now, Katey, there's no time to be doing with
names anymore.'

And I gave you that look again, near upside down it was

and you sighed

and gave a gesture I came to know so well

a mannered way in which you'd slowly close those eyes,
and run your lower lip back and forth along them wee
bumps on your front teeth. Gearing yourself up for some
real wild shite.

'Let's say for argument's sake his name is Joe.'

   Beat.

I heard that

I remember not breathing

I remember thinking

does he know?

How could he know?

I remember you enjoying the fear in my eyes, even if you didn't understand it. I remember the energy you took from it.

'why don't we say Joe, he's here trying to court a girl who barely notices him

no that's too sad for our big Joe here

let's say he gets a little something

by the gents

something chaste between her and him

and now in his mind it's them two all the way to oblivion.

Not that she's feeling that way

cos Joe

look at him

aw Christ would you look at him?

Joe isn't the type you risk ending up with

his brain is all spent muscle and smouldering turf.

Not that it matters.

Cos tonight he's gone. She's gone. All of us, Katey

gone.

Imagine it.

After the bomb

there can be no more of anything

and there's no getting round that. Nor should there be.

You see, Katey, this here's my point.

Nothing matters but the breaking.

Not the who.

Not the why.

Just that we see this fight for the sham that it is.

You see it, don't you?

See that there are people

the very same people who watch you when you walk up the Ormeau Road in the winter dark

people who tell you, you need to be picking some sort of side

and then they show you two sides of the same coin

as if

people

I'm saying

the very same people who finger their moustaches on slow buses

who tell you to fight for them ones or these ones

and then there is me

at the party

who says his name is Diver, and hears your name is Kate

who says there is a solution to all this that no fucker but him has even thought of, and who hears you roll your eyes

who then sits with you in this bar and says that below our table here in the snug, there is the bomb. If we can imagine it. A bomb that waits then ticks then waits then ticks.

And it does tick, Kate, don't think that's just for them Roadrunner cartoons. To tick is its first function.

Listen.

It tells the time. And it'll do that until time comes for each and every one of us.

Our pal from before

fucksake, Katey

I've already forgotten it

want to say Declan or Cormac or'

'Joe'

'Aye

(*Smiling.*) Big Joe.

Well Joe is not wholly dissimilar from the bomb in this respect. He was born to a sheep-shagging culchie

to a long line of sheep-shagging culchies

and is with us this day a perfect cocktail of sheep and man. And whichever species of heart he has inherited it doesn't matter, cos that heart is going to tick and tick just the same as any other the great Ahura Mazda saw fit to wind up for us.

The whole time certain

so monumentally certain

that as long as it can hear itself tick

how could it ever reach the end? It's certain of that. The rational fact of our immortal bodies.

But it will end, Kate.

These bodies we wear are not immortal.

Because to end is our second function.

Our most important function.

Because it clears the way.

All these cultists

wasting it

planting their flags in each other's skulls

they're planting those flags in dust.

Ignoring how simple it could be

that you and me

even Big Joe over there

we are such simple things.'

You reached into my bag and pulled out Joe's envelope. The tear through its body still weeping.

You took a pen and scrawled across him in those big cartoon loops and tails.

Scrawled your name

a number

and then left me there in the rubble of your words

to feel myself breaking

to feel every body in the world breaking with me.

To feel that truth in common.

Wasn't long before I completely fell in with you.

Chucked school, got a job in a big hotel.

Didn't see Shonagh again.

Heard later she opened an eel farm near Lisnaskea.

*

The train to the north coast jolts on its tracks

fields blur into fields

their greens and yellows leaping into the endless blue-white
of the wild sky beyond.

Across the aisle

at a table seat

I can see

there's me and Brendy

from weeks ago

sat having breakfast.

I think 'how did I get all the way over there when I'm right
here?'

and I shouldn't listen

it's none of my business

but I am listening

and there's past Brendy now

smiling through his Weetabix

'what should we call it? While we're waiting.'

And there's me

looking at him like he's after smearing shit on my toast.

'You want to start on with names? Already?'

'No, not a name

just a

a

a noun, like

I'm thinking there should be A Noun

there's something wrong so there is

'saying "it" all the time

it's the size of a pea.'

The train brushes a long hedgerow and I feel each branch
like fingers down my back.

I'm wanting these clowns to shut up

just quiet, please

but I hear me even louder than before.

'Ahh yes

I get you

It's making my tits sore

It's the milkman's baby.'

And there's him saying

'Let me think a while.

'Something better will come. I'm good at this sort of thing.

My gift to you, wife.'

*

I've lost sight

of the border that separates me out

with you so far away all this time

and me so near to something

something

else

maybe

and I don't even mean what they're saying on the news

who knows with all that

and anyway

Christ, this will sound stupid

it will

but seeing it all the time

the way they keep pointing at us

I only just realised I'd never looked, not properly

at the map I'm saying

not until recently

I said this to Brendy and he thought I'd gone loopy

I mean I'd seen it

loads of times

but I'd never really

looked

at the border

how strange it is

that wild line

cutting in and out and round and back on itself

as you would say, Diver

'good for one thing

keeps them cunts on the other side.

Them down there

them that exchanged one empire for another'

you'd say

'We up here

Katey

we break the rocks that will make Ireland

not them

the force of us

of how alive we are

of what that we will bring

they can make neither head nor tail of it.

We are the deluge, Katey

they the floodplain.

We are the only ones on this island who know what our lives are worth.'

Kate takes a deep breath.

So there I was the other week

going about my day

got the washing hung

and the shopping

and Brendy his Easter egg

only the big Snickers for Brendy now

he's a Snickers man, through and through

and then

it's this

feeling it, it's not

I'm not sure

but

it's pain

here

Kate touches her abdomen.

where

pain, I'm saying

pain, the colour

the colour of it running through me

the colour of the heat that night in Pisa

and his skin

and I am feeling

peach

and I know

I know what has happened

and Brendy, he says

'Are you sure?'

and I go to smack him one

but when I turn around he's gone and there's me coming in again

out of the sleet this time

same day though

like a snow storm, you wouldn't believe it for April, blanketing Shaftesbury Square

maybe it's the next day now I'm thinking

and I'm there with this huge medical dictionary out of the library

as if

and in the night

that night

and the next

I'm begging

begging something

but I know

this pain

and Brendy saying

'it could be anything

could be fibroids

a third of women'

which gives him away it does

been talking to this nurse pal he's made at five-a-side

getting some reassurance

just for himself.

'We'll not know until you're seen' he says.

Seen and scanned and pried apart

all to be told something my body has been screaming at me
since day dot.

*

When it finally got too much

hiding with you there in Portbenoney

in that mad wee caravan

like we were in witness protection

every day

watching you watch the water

like you could see the fucking Armada on the horizon

or like it was the ocean itself

like you had to always have your eye on it

or it'd mount the shore and swallow you whole

I said

'I'm going home, Diver.

Mummy and Daddy

Daddy has cooled off

Mummy, she says so

or at least

they're for putting me up

and I'm going to stay with them

and do night school

and take the O levels

and we can't keep going on like this you know we can't.'

And you said nothing.

'who are you even running from anymore?'

And you said nothing.

And I said

'you'll come visit'

and you said nothing.

And I said

'well, I'll come and visit you'

and you said

'An ice cream

and a lazy drive down the promenade on a Sunday evening.'

And you laughed then

crueller than any word you ever laid on me

and I said

'what do you want to happen, Diver?

what do you want from me?'

And you said

'Nothing, fuck off'

   Beat.

And then you said

'I want you in winter. I want you slipped on the ice. I want
you soaked in the wind and the wet. I want you in the bus
shelter at midnight when the last one went through at nine
p.m. and in the dunes in the long marram and in the arcade
playing pool with some smick coked off his face and
throwing raw meat at a sleeping dog'

and I said

'let's write to each other'

and you laughed again

or didn't

all there is now is the feeling of that cold light on my face

the feeling of it empty

like the morning was the thinnest blanket

laid over the night

restless in her crib

and I said

or I want to have said

'I'm serious

deadly serious

so I am

I'm going to write you

and you're going to write me back.'

And your anger changed colour

became a small anger

which I do remember, the shift

because I remember all the shades of your anger

I was their collector

'Fucking

just.

I tell you what.

You ever see a letter from me, Katey

it'll be like that boy

that boy

fucking

Joe

that fella whose name you whimper in your sleep

aye you do

Big Joe who left you for the river.

What a joke.

   Beat.

Time came for that boy long ago, Katey.

   Beat.

Anyone ever hands you a letter from me

then don't even bother looking at it

it'll be just like Joe

there'll be no return address.'

*

I book in at the B&B still feeling the fight with Brendy this morning.

I get my head straight then make my way across town to the address the child bride gave me for Diver.

Kate looks around.

Portbenoney.

As I walk along the seafront I realise how much has changed in the town.

Everything I knew here from ten years ago has been torn down and replaced.

It's all luxury apartments now

cladding gleaming

yet to be licked dull by the salt air.

I look up at the windows and there's not a light in any of them.

It's Easter weekend but it feels like no one is around.

In this whole town

there's probably no one but Diver

he chased them all out

or maybe it's the other way around

they've stopped the trains

and moved the people away

so this new peace that's coming in can really stretch out uninterrupted.

The place where Diver is staying turns out to be a bedsit at the edge of town.

I try the buzzer a few times, but get nothing.

Then this wee woman shuffles up with her shopping

looks at me like I might be about to put a knife to her

and despite her best efforts, I slip in the door behind her before it shuts.

In unsure English she asks who I am, and I say I'm a friend of Diver. Diver.

She nods in a way that tells me she's satisfied I'm not here to set fire to the place.

I move through the building

all the doors I pass are open and I see these are single rooms

just sad little cells.

Going up a floor, I poke my head into the shared kitchen.

There is an ancient muck coating every surface.

A little box TV is shackled high up on the wall

and the news is playing

the contrast is so high

the sight of it is louder than the sound of it

piercing bright images, smiling, shaking hands.

Christ the hands must be for coming off these Brits for all this mad shaking they're having to do.

I come to the door with the number I was given.

I knock.

And I wait a bit.
And I knock again.
And soon I start thinking
if he's in there
if I get in there
and I find him
I'm not seeing that
I'm not
not here
where the river joins the ocean
and I am not seeing that
I will not
and I bang the door
harder
a machine gun tempo
and I say
'Diver.
Diver.
Diver, it's me
Kate
Katey
from
what am I
you know me

I'm here

I came

for a visit

I was visiting anyway

I thought

it's Katey

Diver

it's Katey

open the door.'

I hear something off to my right.

I move back and look down the corridor.

The shopping lady has her door cracked and is watching me.

I take a step towards her and she quickly retreats. I hear a deadbolt lock into place.

I turn back to Diver's door to knock one last time.

But it's open.

The door is open and Diver is there.

Beat.

He's just standing, breathing

his face fixed but his eyes doing their own thing

swivelling

a half-stunned calf, not moving, its stink pouring out.

Then, without saying a word, Diver walks past me towards the kitchen. I follow.

Getting a good look at the shape of him now

long and thin as he ever was, but turned old

fuck, he was always old

but now

older than I expected

I don't know what I expected

but there he is

sagging

like this building

near buckled under something I'm not seeing

and his walk is slow and strange

as if unpractised, as if one foot and then another is a dance
he's only just started to learn.

I take a seat next to a low tower of dishes, fused together in
their filth.

He stands at the sink for a while

maybe listening to that BBC voice droning out of the telly

that voice flattened under the maximum historicity of this
momentous moment for the prostrate people of Northern
Ireland.

Diver is still stood

drenched in the clear white from a fluorescent above.

It picks out the sallow contours of his skin.

The peach.

The heat.

It's a while before I realise he's not doing or saying anything

nothing at all

and I'm just there

watching

watching his back rise and descend as small breaths wash in and out of him.

I wonder if he's gone to sleep

stood there in front of me

so I'm about to ask as much when suddenly he announces

'Somedrink.'

He tries again.

'Something.

To

drink.'

'Yeah

thanks, Diver

just a water.'

Half a look at me on that

a moment of recognition maybe

but he says nothing. He pries a glass cup from the crud and gives it a slow, aimless wipe with his long yellowed fingers.

'Know why I'm here?' I offer.

Diver hands me the cup still empty and then backs away.

He looks past me at the window

as if suspicious of something out there.

I turn around and see our reflections in the glass and the dark night.

We're staring out like we're waiting for the flash to go off a portrait of a woman and her man

reunited after a long war.

I turn back to Diver, but he keeps his eyes on that darkness.

'The wee girl you've been seeing

she called me.

Diver.

She's been trying to reach you.

You scared her.

You made her think you'd done something to yourself.'

Though his expression hasn't changed, tears are now
tracing his cheek bones.

I think of his nana, knelt beside him in her green kimono.

She'll have passed by now, I wonder when that happened.

'Diver?'

He stirs.

His eyes fix on me.

Suddenly he's close, rearing up.

I get to my feet and that's enough to make him back away.

'Diver' I say

'Diver

listen to me'

He's mumbling, agitated.

He comes at me again.

I move past him, get out, close the door behind me.

I stand there, on the other side

my heart a siren pealing through me

and through the door

the noise he's making

suddenly

a terrible screeching

it hooks in

the heat of his blood in my body again

and all our memories breaking across the floor of me.

Down the corridor the neighbour has appeared

and is beckoning me to come.

So I let go of the handle and lunge towards her.

She pulls me into her room and deadbolts us in.

She points at the lock and gives it two thumbs up.

Says to me 'strong, safe.'

Pause.

This wee woman spends the next twenty minutes with her ear pressed tight to the door. When she finally hears Diver collapse back in his room, she takes me by the hand and bustles me out and on to the street.

I turn to thank her, but she's already hurried back inside.

When I land back in the B&B I check the time. If I left now I could still make the last train.

But I don't move.

I sit.

I sit on the bed and I listen.

And I feel like I can still hear Diver

that screeching

calling me.

Beat.

I phone the child bride and relay the good news.

She is relieved.

'Oh thank fuck for that, Katey.

Sure give him my love.'

Beat.

Then I call Brendy.

I tell him I'm having to stay just a wee bit longer.

I tell him it turns out there's no trains tomorrow, it being Easter Sunday.

So now it'll be Monday I'm back.

Sorry about lunch. Sorry to your sisters. Sorry to their kids.

He's saying never mind all that.

He's saying the scan is Tuesday.

I mumble an apology.

He's saying he's worried sick.

'I can't believe you, Kate

why aren't you here with me?'

Christ, wee girl, I don't even know who you are anymore.

I go to answer but I feel the pain come again

I feel it twist through me

unlike anything I've felt before

so I slam the phone down

I don't want to give Brendy the satisfaction of hearing it in my voice.

I lie back on the bed and switch the TV on, waiting for the pain to pass, but it doesn't

instead it slowly roots in and becomes an ache in every part of me.

I try hard to focus on the voices from across the room

on their endless celebration of our escape into peace

but my mind begins to cycle in step with the throb of my body

between pain and exhaustion

between Diver and this new future

as it is now

not as it was then

a vision of Ireland

pressed flat beneath the rock

desperate to be released

    Beat.

(*Disgust.*) They come and they *give* us peace.

    Beat.

After all this time

give it to us

as if it was easy

after eight hundred years telling us every day we're no good

that it's in our bones

how could we ever be good

when we hang around with scumbags like him.

   Beat.

Before

before Diver there is nothing.

And in that nothing there is Joseph.

Big Joe.

Showing up every night behind my eyes

saying

'I've been walking.'

saying

'I've been walking for so long.'

stopping me along the embankment

saying

'My feet hurt.'

The waves on the Lagan singing at him to come back in the water. And him saying

'The rocks down here

I keep cutting my feet on them'

and then louder

'There are cuts on the cuts on my feet'

And I see

the river bed below

them rocks like shark teeth

coming up

cutting him

his sweet little feet.

I follow as they bleed into the river

and he's saying

'Kate

why don't you ever write me back?'

And here's my memory turning with the water and
knocking a new shape to things past

here's Daddy

not ever looking me in the eye

saying

'The stench, on your clothes, in your room where
everything piles up and the window never opens.

What is going on with you, wee girl?'

And fuck me

these great cliffs on the north side of Ormeau Park stand
arched above me now

and here's Big Joe lying in the shallow

his mind trickling towards the sea

towards him

towards his mouth

before

before there was all them guns

and these hills was diamonds

and the bogs held only muck

and the language on our tongues was our own

and way back

if we go way back

there was wee Katey

cutting about with wee Shonagh

the first woman and the first friend

and the worst the Girl Guides had ever seen

and the bomb now

where is it?

I can hear it

tick tick tick tick

I imagine buildings

big brick bucks

I imagine my body

I imagine

this could have been once

it could have been loads of times

the tide tucking me in

the land bleeding moonlight

the only thing that used to scare me

everyone said this

was this idea of things falling down

everything bigger than me

everything

I imagined the city centre

all them buildings

made me think

what if they got tired? The buildings. The bricks. What if they wanted to sleep?

I was always wanting sleep

and I was only wee

so why not

the thoughts in my head

the crushing

not fast, not

but slow

slowly down on top of me

and this one time

I think, it could have been

but this one time I'm in bed and the terror is just

huge

the way the house is cracking above me

I was looking up at the ceiling and I could see it, slowly, moving, coming down.

But Daddy, he came when I called, and he says to me 'it's just the man on the moon.'

Daddy. I loved him. The strength of him. Calming me. Saying

'The man on the moon is having a party, Katey. He's dancing up there.'

But that ceiling was so low

slowly

the tip of my nose

and Daddy, his back full flat against it

pushing up

hard as he could.

God I loved him

so much it is all across me still

his face bleeding lamplight

and I loved him I did I loved him

silly with it even now.

But then Diver came.

And me and him, we took me somewhere else.

And Daddy

   Beat.

And yet here's Joseph our beautiful lamb so he is

just in pieces

and yet here's wee Katey and her gang of Gilnahirk Girls on
the escalator

giving the finger

and giggling to each other

and eating fistfuls of bird bones

spitting them back over

these hills full of diamonds.

And slowly

down on me

the tip of my nose

it doesn't sound like dancing

and he says to me

'that's because it's so far above us, Katey.

From a whole other world.'

Face bleeding moonlight

lungs bleeding water

and

and

and then

Beat.

When I stopped by for my things and told Daddy that me
and Diver were going to be staying together in the city, he
said Diver and his kind were scum

dragging us back

our whole nation

and I should know better and I was raised better and I was
a stupid bitch

and then he went up to his room to sulk and fold shirts.

Mummy said he wasn't going to come back while I was still
hanging about

and she was right

he stayed up there a hundred thousand years and folded
them two shirts of his so many times and so tightly they
ended up fitting inside one matchbox.

So I left.

Act Three

The next day.

Easter Sunday.

I go where I know Diver will find me.

Sat in the only pub in town that isn't the other pub in town.

Eventually he arrives

cleaned up in that way he could

sure, your eyes would not recognise him.

He spots me and slinks over.

'Katey Regan.

What about ye?

Or wait

didn't you get hitched sometime back?

you'll be Mrs Such-and-Such'

(*Flat.*) 'No. I kept my name'

Diver claps loudly.

'Good on ye

that's what I like to hear

no fucker is putting his name over you

sure it would only burn up in your atmosphere.'

I take a drink, but say nothing.

He tries me again.

(*Quiet, testing the water.*) 'I think I saw you last night.
In a dream.'
(*Resolute.*) 'I certainly saw you, Diver'
His eyes fall to his lap.
(*Deflated.*) 'That so.
We must be dreaming the same dreams.'
Then he looks at me

   Diver grins.

says to me
'Mine's still a rum and Coke when you're going up.'
And after two or three of them rums
I tell Diver about me and Brendy
I tell him about waiting for the scan
and the pain
the pain last night
the pain still, right now
I tell him it doesn't even matter I'm drinking tonight
I'm sure
I'm empty
and Diver holds my hand
and after two or three again
he says all those years ago
he wasn't always thinking right
except when he was thinking about me
and after three or three more

we're out on our arses

on the beach

it's biting

but we're laughing

and I remember how his laugh could feel in me when he wanted it to feel like it was everything

and it does

it is everything

and we are

we're hooting

because he's just claimed to have invented hummus

and I'm trying to say

what the fuck are you talking about

and he's all

'no no I'm not saying

I'm not saying I made it up completely

that's not what I'm saying

that was the Arabs, wasn't it?'

And I'm fucking laughing so hard

I'm snorting like

and he's still saying

'no no

that's not it'

that in fact he was the one who brought hummus to Ireland

so in effect

invented

and then he leans over and kisses me

and I kiss him

and we kiss

we

like before

and I whisper a sorry to Brendy.

I am sorry

but my sorrow is only this whisper.

Because I had to

I'm so straight these days

normally

I've been

even that time I wasn't

I didn't

but now

I kiss and he kisses

and the night is nipping hard at my bare arms

and of course Diver, he tries to make it more

rolling on and off me like I'm a lump of dough

getting sand in my socks

and I push him back

and he tries to force it

hands heavy

but I go limp

automatic

muscle memory

and he feels that

and he stops

sits up

looks away from me.

And then

after a minute

he says

'All this

have you been been watching it, Katey?

On the news?'

I laugh because the way he says it

it's like I might have missed the whole peace agreement
thing that's been happening lately.

> *Diver ignores Kate's laugh and tries to push on with
> what he's saying.*

'All this they're doing

to fix us.

It's

> *Diver is struggling.*

not how I saw it.

Not how I saw it at all.

Going out with a whimper

with a pen'

and then he throws out his arms

towards the night

and he looks at them

like he has something written on them

something he was going to say

something that would unlock the truth of this pain in me.

But he says nothing. He has nothing.

I feel only his desperation

wanting me to see myself in him

to lie with him here in the rubble

like I lied with him before.

But there are these years in the way

and I am

I am more I am

more than I was then

before

with all that Diver breath on my Katey neck.

There is just too much of me now.

Too much of me breaking for him to get a proper grip.

I look at him. I can see there is barely any border between
him and the black water in front of us.

I see time is coming for him.

And he knows I know that.

So he turns his face to the void

away from the pain of my gaze.

Pause.

It's only a few hours later that I leave Portbenoney to catch the morning train to Belfast.

Diver surprises me at the station. His mood has changed completely.

He does a little dance on the spot.

The tiled floor stretches out under our feet.

All the wet that's been walked in gleams back at us

like we are Fred and Ginger here to make it sing.

I think about the pain I feel

that colour running through me

the peach

the heat.

As the tannoy announces my train arriving, Diver pulls me close and thanks me

says to me

'Katey

I feel so much better for having seen you again

you are just what I needed

I'm a new man'

I hear the screech of the train pulling in to the station

and I feel Diver screeching behind that kitchen door.

Suddenly he kisses me again

this time the cheek

and I recoil

but he leans in, tightens his grip and whispers

'I know we could have had one

one of our own

back at the beginning.'

I freeze.

'Sometimes I think

if it had happened that way

I could have stopped

I could have been different'

Every part of me is frozen and cannot move.

His breath against my ear is gasping and wet.

'But then I remember myself

and I know it couldn't have ever been any other way

because I can only break things, Katey.

That's all I've ever been good for.'

A ticket collector shouts a last call for the train to Belfast.
I try to break free, but Diver holds on.

'I know you think you're the same as me

but you're not, Katey'

Every cell of me is alive with revulsion and pushing against
him.

'Because I heard something

last night

when you let me near

I pressed my ear on you

and I heard it

and whatever that is you've got

I have no word for it'

I pull myself free and run for the train.

At the barrier I glance back

and see Diver stood

waist deep in the wet floor

smiling up at me.

*

The train shuffles by the sea and as it turns in towards the
first fields I move through the empty carriage to watch the
ocean disappear.

Out there, bobbing in the water

I make out a line of buoys

marking something

marking

   Sudden panic.

What am I doing?

I shouldn't be leaving

not now

I should be there

I should be breaking

there

in the waves

   Calmer.

but the track turns again and I must have forgot because
I'm soon on the sofa with the TV on loud

and it's one of them shows they make over there

with them types they get to go on the TV
drinking white wine and tutting at peasants.
And then I sleep.
And it feels like the first sleep in years.
  Beat.
When I wake it is nearly morning
and there is a blanket over me.
Brendy.
I move to get up
and
I feel it
I know
I know there is blood
and I look
and yes
some
not a lot
but it's on the sofa as well
Jesus wept
and I go into the kitchen to get something to clean it with
but I don't know where
I don't
Brendy
fucksake
he's always moving things and reorganising

never happy leaving things how they are

how they are meant to be

and it does my head in

and I nearly go and wake him to give him a row

but

I don't

I sit there

and I

I am alone

and it's awful.

*

Way back at the beginning

another of those stays at Nana's house on Jerusalem Street.

Now this is a funny one

can't believe I nearly went all this way without it.

Across the road

one night

I remember

the gunshot

the scream

two points on the map unfolding

linked events

but further apart than you would have thought

the gunshot

I woke and then slept again

fitful

and then the scream

a woman screaming

so much later

that sticks in my mind

like she'd had to pull it up from some part of her unknown

some part low and terrible.

A flash of light

then so much later

thunder

that distance.

And then out on the street in the night

all of us wrapped in a single bedsheet

offering witness

sure, there were already young fellas out kicking a ball

as if the gunshot had spooked the clocks

so that they fell back into the night

a gift of another hour before school.

On the other side of the road

a door flings open

and a weird light floods the dark

and with it

your woman

yelling

'where is my boy'

yelling

'where is my boy'

and out into the city

a mess she was

her son smeared all down her jammies

she's walking

where?

Fucking

sure she has nowhere to go, the mad woman.

At this hour.

Just wailing and stumbling.

And the men they followed.

The husbands and the sons.

Knowing they should do something

but not knowing what can be done

so instead a distance

a slow prowl

hunters out after a wounded beast

limping away from the herd

and I

I'm over the road

and I

what am I doing?

By myself

at her door

into the home now empty

the light in the hallway

a body there

her son

I recognised

his hands

small, strong

his sweet little feet

a body younger than mine

but no head on him

that was the thing.

And a rifle near by.

A strangeness to see

death

in amongst all the other death

but this one laid out neatly for me and only me

no before

no after

no meaning or explanation.

Not like the movies

much

duller.

I made sure and turned the light off.

Saved her the meter.

And I stood there

in the dark

and felt

I think

a kind of peace.

And then back in my bed and I slept.

We are such simple things.

*

Brendy takes the morning off work to be with me.

It's still dark when we arrive at the hospital.

There's a clandestine feel to it as we wander the campus looking for maternity.

The nurse is waiting on the ramp outside, holding a coffee close to her chest.

Sure aren't we lucky, she's opening the shop early for us

and oh Christ

let this be done now.

Once I'm changed and on the bed I feel for the briefest of moments this

hope

I hear a voice

my own voice

but from before

before

ages before

so far before it's coming in from the future

and

I hear

I think I hear

faintly

tick

tick

but as she rolls the paddle over my belly I watch the screen
and see only fuzz

I look back at her and she is grimacing

muttering to herself

I hear

'Now that's not what we want'

I am breaking

'not what we want at all'

I am the river burst its banks and dragging clumps of black
earth out to sea.

We wait while she leaves to find a chaperone so she can do
an internal scan.

Brendy squeezes my shoulder.

Slowly

calmly

I rip his arm from its socket and fling it at the wall.

He adjusts his position and squeezes my shoulder with his
other hand.

She returns in a fluster and asks if we're happy to go on
ahead without the chaperone

it being Easter break

everyone's holidays all at once

and that Christina off on maternity leave still
and I look at her and I'm sure I am screaming
but somehow she isn't hearing me
and Brendy
being now only one-armed and wise to the danger
he says to her we just need this done
and she nods and is in me
I tell you now
with some force
with this huge intergalactic dildo-looking thing
fuck me
and the pain of it
the humiliation
and Brendy sees my body jolt
and he squeezes
he squeezes for dear life
and I know there is love there but I can't reach it
and then she mutters
'nope, not over there'
and then she mutters
'no no no.'
And then she stops.
Brendy hasn't seen it yet
but I see her
her eyes are closed and she has stopped.

And then

inside me

I hear a single terrible note

bright

clear

and then

'There we are

sure baby was just playing hide and seek on us

weren't you, baby'

and I don't know what she means

but then she swivels the screen, and I can see it flicker
where she's pointing

and she says that's a heartbeat

a strong heartbeat

'well done, baby'

and I say no you daft bitch

that's a whole other world

and I squeeze Brendy back

and I look at him

and he's crying

and we're crying

and this nurse is checking her watch

tick

tick

tick

At home Brendy just does not know what to do with himself.

He tidies the kitchen

then the spare room

sure why not, let's do the kitchen again.

I sit on the bed and feel the sun through the window and the tree just outside

the light pushes through the branches and nestles in streaks between the shadows across my belly

and there within me, something else

and I'm trying to name it

but before I can Brendy trots in

quick kisses on the crown of my head

puts a letter beside me

says it was on the floor under my coat

must have fallen out when I was hanging it up

and then is away, once more, to descale the kettle.

I pick up the letter and squint at it.

And in the hall the phone rings, Brendy shouts that he'll get it

(*Distracted.*) 'No, wait.'

The letter

it's small, feels like nothing in my hand, and I'm looking and

you know it's weird

because for some reason

I can't figure out how to get in

94

it's hilarious actually

and the phone is still ringing

and the letter

and Brendy shouts again

I'm turning the envelope round and round

and I start to see

this writing on one side

the phone stops ringing, but then starts again

and the writing on the envelope

these cartoon loops and tails

that round, hurried scrawl

and I hear a distant click as Brendy picks up the phone

and the peach

no

the wet yellow

and Brendy is saying 'Hello'

but his voice is somewhere else entirely now

in another time

because I'm moving

swimming back along the tracks

the water on one side

this empty space on the other

I'm in the station yesterday

a whisper in my ear

a hand in my coat pocket

the force of this letter, the force of you, pushing

and I hear Brendy faintly in that other land, so serious sounding, so sad

I look across the room

and I see a void

and through it

our first night

right there in the snug as the ceiling comes down on us.

Your hand here

right here

the small of my back.

You called it the bodyguard's touch.

You said

you will see that we are all just sculptors, Katey.

We are breaking all the time

breaking the rock to reveal what is underneath.

To carve out some kind of paradise.

Beat.

But no. That's not what it was with you.

It was just destruction with no end in sight.

It was just your name scrawled across a letter from a dead boy

and I see now

in my hands

it is the same letter

it always has been

so on the bed in this room where I hold my daughter with one fist

I take your envelope in the other

and

I squeeze

and

I *squeeze*

and I open my palm

and nothing of you remains.

   Beat.

And I see now

I see before

truly I do

I see Joe

I see Shonagh

I see you, Daddy

because it was you, Daddy, before anything

you were always telling me I let you down.

That I was meant to be better than this.

And when you were about to pass

in the same hospital where my daughter will be born

lying there with your lungs full of water

you looked at me and you said you loved me.

But it's only now I know how both things can be true.

Because you let me down more than anyone and I loved you more than anyone.

Before everything

me and you

we had this love in common.

We are all such simple things.

And what I've got in me now

what I've got coming next

sure when she goes

it won't matter where any of us were sitting

it won't matter that any of us still dream and wake and cry out in the night

it won't matter that the river is calling me

is still calling me

now

with peace creeping over these hills

and my body still breaking

because it has to be breaking for her to be freed

I know that now

and because just the thought of her has already broken this world

in the way we couldn't

and carved it into something new

in a way we could never conceive

untouched by

before

before

before

oh Christ

before

carving it in me even now

I can feel it

carving something

good

that is good

finally

good.

End.